Other books by Francis A. Schaeffer

Escape from Reason
The God Who Is There
Death in the City
Pollution and the Death of Man
The Church at the End of the 20th Century
The Mark of the Christian
The Church before the Watching World
He Is There and He Is Not Silent
True Spirituality
Genesis in Space and Time
The New Super-Spirituality
Back to Freedom and Dignity
Basic Bible Studies
Art and the Bible
No Little People
Everybody Can Know (Francis and Edith Schaeffer)

2 contents,
2 realities
Francis A. Schaeffer

InterVarsity Press
Downers Grove, Illinois 60515

InterVarsity Press
is the book publishing
division of Inter-Varsity
Christian Fellowship.

ISBN 0-87784-309-0

Printed in the United
States of America

Publisher's foreword

What is the Christian's task in the world today? Some say evangelism—spreading the good news of Jesus Christ to a lost and despairing world. That's the task.

Unfortunately, this genuine and crucial part of the Christian life often gets separated from the rest of life. To train himself in evangelism, the Christian turns to "technique" books and "how-to" pamphlets, many of which encourage a mechanical approach. As a result, evangelism sometimes becomes stuffing the gospel down an unconverted throat.

Biblical evangelism is not, after all, simply the propagation of a canned message plus the call for a decision. Nor is it the manipulation of people with the latest technique of psychology. We are to treat our fellow man with respect. Each person has dignity, and, because all of us are made in the image of God, we are not to manipulate each other—even for the "good" end of salvation.

Our failure to see this results from our failure to recognize evangelism as only a part—a natural part—of our whole posture as Christians. The lordship of Christ extends to every area of our lives. It relates to doctrine and theology, world view and lifestyle, faith and practice, our attitude to race and our attitude to economics. To put it in Francis Schaeffer's terms, being a Christian in the world today involves two contents and two realities. It is only in such a framework that evangelism can be rightly understood and practiced.

This pamphlet is the text of the address which Francis A. Schaeffer presented at the International Congress on World Evangelization, Lausanne, Switzerland, July 1974. It represents the core of his message to the church today. Added as an appendix is an essay on race and economics; this essay, which expands some of the material treated in the major address, first appeared in Christianity Today. We are pleased to make both available to a wider audience.

THERE ARE FOUR THINGS WHICH I THINK ARE AB-
SOLUTELY NECESSARY IF WE AS CHRISTIANS ARE
TO MEET THE NEED OF OUR AGE AND THE OVER-
WHELMING PRESSURE WE ARE INCREASINGLY FAC-
ING. THEY ARE TWO CONTENTS AND TWO REALITIES.

The First Content: Sound Doctrine

The first content is clear doctrinal content concerning the
central elements of Christianity. There is no use talking
about meeting the threat of the coming time or fulfilling our
calling in the midst of the last quarter of the twentieth century unless we consciously help each other to have a clear
doctrinal position. We must have the courage to make no

compromise with liberal theology and especially neo-orthodox existential theology.

Christianity is a specific body of truth; it is a system and we must not be ashamed of the word *system*. There is truth and we must hold that truth. There will be borderline things in which we have differences among ourselves, but on the central issues there must be no compromise.

Evangelicals can fall into something which really is not very far from existential theology without knowing it. One form of such "evangelical existentialism" is the attitude, if not the words, "Don't ask questions, just believe." This sort of attitude was always wrong, but it is doubly wrong today when we are surrounded with a monolithic consensus which divides reason from non-reason, and always puts religious things in the area of non-reason. We must call each other away from this idea. It is not more spiritual to believe without asking questions. It is not more biblical. It is less biblical and eventually it will be less spiritual because the whole man will not be involved. Consequently, in our evangelism, in our personal work, in our young people's work, in our ministry wherever we are, those of us who are preachers and are preaching, those of us who are teachers and are teaching and those of us who are evangelists must be absolutely determined not to fall into the trap of saying or implying, "Don't ask questions, just believe." It must be the whole man who comes to understand that the gospel is truth and believes because he is convinced on the basis of good and sufficient reason that it is truth.

Moreover, we must be very careful to emphasize content in our messages. How much content will depend upon the people with whom we are working. In a university setting, the content will be slightly different than in a situation where people are not as educated. Nevertheless, whether we work with a man or woman who is not as educated or whether we work with an intellectual, in all instances, the gospel we preach must be rich in content. Certainly, we must be very careful not to fall into the cheap solution (which seems so fascinating at first) of just moving people to make decisions without their really knowing what they are making a decision about. We in L'Abri have had people come to us who have "accepted Christ as Savior" but are not even sure that God exists. They have never been confronted with the question of the existence of God. The acceptance of Christ as Savior was a thing abstracted. It had an insufficient content. In reality it was just another kind of trip.

Likewise, in a Christian school or college we can try just to religiously move the students on the basis of something apart from the intellect, separated from the academic disciplines and the whole of study. We must say no to this.

What we need to do is to understand our age to be an age of very subtle religious and political manipulation, manipulation by cool communication, communication without content. And as we see all these things, we must lean against them. We have a message of content; there is a system to Christianity. It is not *only* a system, true enough; it is not a dead scholasticism, true enough; but it *is* a system in that the person who accepts Christ as his Savior must do so in the midst of the understanding that prior to the creation of the world a personal God on the high level of trinity existed. And if they "accept Christ as their Savior" and do not understand that God exists as an infinite-personal God and do not understand that man has been made in the image of God and has value, and do not understand that man's dilemma is not metaphysical because he is small but moral because man revolted against God in a space-time Fall, in all probability they are not saved. If we "evangelize" by asking for such "acceptance of Christ as Savior," all we have done is to guarantee they will soon drift away and become harder to reach than ever. Not everybody must know everything—nobody knows everything; if we waited to be saved until we knew everything, nobody would ever be saved—but that is a very different thing from deliberately or thoughtlessly diminishing the content.

Another way to fall into an "evangelical existentialism" is to treat the first half of Genesis the way the existential theologian treats the whole Bible. The first half of Genesis is history, space-time history, the Fall is a space-time Fall, or we have no knowledge of what Jesus came to die for and we have no way to understand that God is really a good God. Our whole answer to evil rests upon the historic, space-time Fall. There was a time before man revolted against God. The internal evidence of Genesis and the external evidences (given in the New Testament by the way the New Testament speaks of the first half of Genesis) show that the first half of Genesis is really meant to be space-time history. We must understand that here we are dealing with history—that is, space and time, the warp and woof of history.

In relationship to this is the danger of diminishing the content of the gospel in a reverse fashion. Bible-believing Christians who stand against the liberal theologian when he would say there are no absolutes in the Bible can make the opposite mistake by adding other elements as though they were equally absolute. In other words, the absolutes of the Word of God can be destroyed in both directions. That is, the liberal theologian can say, "After all, there is no such thing as an absolute, and specifically the Bible does not give absolutes," or the evangelical can reach over into the middle-class standards and say, "These standards are equal to the absolutes of the Word of God."

The obvious illustration is how the church treats the hippie or a person dressed in this different way. Young people come to us at L'Abri from the ends of the earth, become Christians, and go home and then try to find a Bible-believing church that will accept them without all the change of lifestyle. I do not mean they try to retain a drug life or a promiscuous sex life which would be against the Word of God. I mean, for example, the way they dress or talk. It is one of my greatest sorrows. The evangelical church often will not accept the person with his lifestyle unless it fits into the middle-class norm in that particular geographical location. And unhappily, we often do not realize what we have done when we do this. It is not only a lack of love. We have destroyed the absolutes of the Word of God by making something else equal to God's absolutes.

If you ask me why the evangelical church has so often been weak in the question of race in the past, I think it was the same. We were surrounded by a culture that had racial prejudices and did not look at all men as equal, and we allowed this to infiltrate the church. We made taboos apart from and even against the Word of God, and we held them to be equal with the absolutes of the Bible.[1] But to exalt a cultural norm to an absolute is even more destructive today because we are surrounded by a totally relativistic society. As we make other things equal to the absolutes of the Word of God, it may not be more sinful in the sight of God than it was in the past, but it is more destructive. Consequently, when we talk about content, we are talking about something very practical indeed. We must have a strong, strong doctrinal content.

And as we have a strong doctrinal content, we must practice the content, practice the truth we say we believe. We must exhibit to our own children and to the watching world that we take truth seriously. It will not do in a relativistic age to say that we believe in truth and fail to *practice that truth* in places where it may be observed and where it is costly. We, as Christians, say we believe that truth exists. We say we have truth from the Bible. And we say we can give that truth to other men in propositional, verbalized form and they may have that truth. This is exactly what the gospel claims and this is what we claim. But then we are surrounded by a relativistic age. Do you think for a moment we will have credibility if we say we believe the truth and yet *do not practice the truth in religious matters*? If we do not do this, we cannot expect for a moment that the tough-minded, twentieth-century young person, including our

---

[1]The appendix to the present essay enlarges on this topic.

own young people, will take us seriously when we say "here is truth" when they are surrounded by a totally monolithic consensus that truth does not exist.

Consider an example in the academic world. One girl who was teaching in one of the major universities of Britain was a real Christian and very bright. She was teaching in a sociology department whose head was a behaviorist, and he told her she had to teach in the framework of behaviorism or lose her post. Suddenly she was confronted with the question of the practice of truth. She said no, she could not teach behaviorism, and she lost her post. This is what I mean by practicing truth when it is costly. And this will come in many, many places and in many, many ways. It will come in the area of sexual life form, being surrounded by permissive sexualists and asexuality. We must be careful by the grace of God to practice what we say the Bible teaches, the one-man, one-woman relationship, or we are destroying the truth that we say we believe.

But nowhere is practicing the truth more important than in the area of religious cooperation. If I say that Christianity is really eternal truth, and the liberal theologian is wrong— so wrong that he is teaching that which is contrary to the Word of God—and then on any basis (including for the sake of evangelism) I am willing publicly to act as though that man's religious position is the same as my own, I have destroyed the practice of truth which my generation can *expect* from me and which it will *demand* of me if I am to have credibility. How will we have a *credibility* in a relativistic age if we practice religious cooperation with men who in their books and lectures make very plain that they believe nothing (or practically nothing) of the content set forth in Scripture?

Incidentally, almost certainly if we have a latitudinarianism in religious cooperation, the next generation will have a latitudinarianism in doctrine, and specifically a weakness toward the Bible. We are seeing this happen in parts of evangelicalism as well. We must have the courage to take a clear position.

But let us beware. We certainly must not take every one of our small secondary distinctives and elevate them to be the point where we refuse to have fellowship on any level with those who do not hold them. It is the central things of the Word of God which make Christianity Christianity. These we must hold tenaciously, and, even when it is costly for us and even when we must cry, we must maintain that there is not only an antithesis of truth but an antithesis that is observable in practice. Out of a loyalty to the infinite-personal God who is there and who has spoken in Scripture and out of compassion for our own young people and others, we who are evangelicals dare not take a halfway position concerning truth or the practice of truth.

Thus, with regard to the first content there are three things to recognize: first, there must be a strong emphasis on content; second, there must be a strong emphasis on the propositional nature of the Bible, especially the early chapters of Genesis; and third, there must be a strong emphasis on the practice of truth. We can talk about methods, we can stir each other up, we can call each other to all kinds of action, but unless it is rooted in a strong Christian base in the area of content and the practice of truth, we build on sand

and add to the confusion of our day.

Second Content: Honest Answers to Honest Questions
The second content is that Christianity is truth, and we must give honest answers to honest questions. Christianity is truth, truth that God has told us, and if it is truth it can answer questions.

There is no dichotomy in the Bible between the intellectual and cultural on the one hand and the spiritual on the other. But often there has been a strong platonic emphasis in evangelicalism, a strong tendency to divide man into two parts—his spiritual nature and everything else. We must take that conception like a piece of baked clay, break it in our hands and throw it away, and consciously reject the platonic element which has been added to Christianity. God made the whole man; the whole man is redeemed in Christ, and after we are Christians the lordship of Christ covers the whole man. That includes his so-called spiritual things and his intellectual, creative and cultural things; it includes his law, his sociology and psychology; it includes every single part and portion of a man and his being.

The Bible does not suggest that there is something distinct in man which is spiritual and that the rest of man is unrelated to the commands and norms of God. There is nothing in the Bible which would say, "Never mind the intellectual, never mind the cultural. We will follow the Bible in the spiritual realm, but we will take the intellectual and the creative and put them aside. They are not important."

If Christianity is truth as the Bible claims, it must touch every aspect of life. If I draw a pie and that pie comprises the whole of life, Christianity will touch every slice. In every sphere of our lives Christ will be our Lord and the Bible will be our norm. We will stand under the Scripture. It is not that the "spiritual" is under Scripture while the intellectual and creative are free from it.

Consider the ministry of Paul. Paul went to the Jews, and what happened as he talked to them? They asked Paul questions, and he answered. He went to the non-Jews, the Gentiles, and they asked him questions, and he answered. He went into the marketplace, and there his ministry was a ministry of discussion, of giving honest answers to honest questions. He went to Mars Hill and he gave honest answers to honest questions. There are three places in the Bible where Paul was speaking to the man without the Bible (that is, to the Gentiles) without the man with the Bible (the Jew) being present. The first was at Lystra and his discussion there was cut short. Then we find him on Mars Hill where they asked questions and Paul answered; this too was cut short. But one place, happily, where he was not cut short is in the first two chapters of the book of Romans. And there we find carried out exactly the same kind of "argumentation" that he began at Lystra and on Mars Hill.

Many Christians think that 1 Corinthians speaks against the use of the intellect. But it does not. What 1 Corinthians speaks against is a man's pretending to be autonomous, drawing from his own wisdom and his own knowledge without recourse to the revelation of the Word of God. It is a humanistic, rationalistic intellectualism—a wisdom that is generated from man himself as opposed to the teaching of the Scripture—that we must stand against with all our hearts. Paul was against the early gnosticism, wherein a man could be saved merely on the basis of such knowledge. Paul did answer questions. He answered questions wherever they arose.

Consider the ministry of our Lord Jesus himself. What was his ministry like? He was constantly answering questions. Of course they were different kinds of questions from those which arose in the Greek and Roman world, and therefore his discussion was different. But as far as his practice was concerned, he was a man who answered questions, this Jesus Christ, this Son of God, this second person of the Trinity, our Savior and our Lord. But someone will say, "Didn't he say that to be saved you have to be as a little child?" Of course, he did. But did you ever see a little child who didn't ask questions? People who use this argument must never have listened to a little child or been one! My four children gave me a harder time with their endless flow of questions than university people ever have. Jesus did not mean that coming as a little child simply meant making an upper-story leap. What Jesus was talking about is that the little child, when he has an adequate answer, accepts the answer. He has the simplicity of not having a built-in grid whereby, regardless of the validity of the answer, he rejects it. And that is what rationalistic man, humanistic man, does.

Christianity demands that we have enough compassion to learn the questions of our generation. The trouble with too many of us is that we want to be able to answer these questions instantly, as though we could take a funnel, put it in one ear and pour in the facts and then go out and regurgitate them and win all the discussions. It cannot be. Answering questions is hard work. Can you answer all the questions? No, but you must try. Begin to listen with compassion. Ask what this man's questions really are and try to answer. And if you don't know the answer, try to go some place or read and study to find some answers.

Not everybody is called to answer the questions of the intellectual, but when you go down to the shipyard worker you have a similar task. My second pastorate was with shipyard workers, and I tell you they have the same questions as the university man. They just do not articulate them the same way.

Answers are not salvation. Salvation is bowing and accepting God as Creator and Christ as Savior. I must bow twice to become a Christian. I must bow and acknowledge that I am not autonomous; I am a creature created by the Creator. And I must bow and acknowledge that I am a guilty sinner who needs the finished work of Christ for my salvation. And there must be the work of the Holy Spirit. Nonetheless, what I am talking about is our responsibility to have enough compassion to pray and do the hard work which is necessary to answer the honest questions. Of course, we are not to study only cultural and intellectual issues. We ought to study them and the Bible and in both ask for the help of the Holy Spirit.

It is not true that every intellectual question is a moral dodge. There are honest intellectual questions and **somebody must be able to answer them. Maybe not everybody in your church or your young poeple's society can answer them, but the church should be training men and women who can. Our theological seminaries should be committed to this too. It is part of what Christian education ought to be all about.

The Bible puts a tremendous emphasis on content with which the mind can deal. In 1 John we are told what we should do if a spirit or a prophet knocks on our door tonight. If a prophet or spirit knocks on your door, how do you know whether or not he is from God? I have a great respect for the occult, especially after the things we have seen and fought and wrestled against in L'Abri. If a spirit comes, how do you judge him? Or if a prophet comes, how do you judge him? John says, "Beloved, believe not every spirit, but test the spirits whether they are of God: because many false prophets are gone out into the world. Hereby know you the Spirit of God: Every spirit that confesses that Jesus Christ has come in the flesh is of God" (1 Jn. 4:1-2).

Now that is a very nice answer; it has two halves. First, it means Jesus had an eternal pre-existence as the second person of the Trinity, and then it means he came in the flesh. When a prophet or a spirit comes to you, the test of whether he should be accepted or rejected is not the experience that the spirit or prophet gives you. Nor is it the strength of the emotion which the spirit or the prophet gives you. Nor is it any special outward manifestations that the spirit or the prophet may give you. The basis of accepting the spirit or prophet—*and the basis of Christian fellowship*—is Christian doctrine. There is no other final test. Satan can counterfeit and he will.

I am not speaking against emotion in itself. Of course

there should be emotion. I am saying that you cannot trust your emotions or the strength of your emotions or the boost your emotions give you when you stand in the presence of the spirit or the prophet. This does not prove for one moment whether he is from God or the devil or simply from himself. And the same is true with Christian fellowship. These are to be tested, says the Word of God, at the point at which the mind can work and that is on the basis of Christian doctrine.

So there are two contents, the content of a clear doctrinal position and the content of honest answers to honest questions. I now want to talk about two realities.

The First Reality: True Spirituality
The first reality is spiritual reality. Let us emphasize again as we have before, we believe with all our hearts that Christian truth can be presented in propositions, and that anybody who diminishes the concept of the propositionalness of the Word of God is playing into twentieth-century, non-Christian hands. But, and it is a great and strong *but*, the end of Christianity is not the repetition of mere propositions. Without the proper propositions you cannot have that which should follow. But after having the correct propositions the end of the matter is to love God with all our hearts and souls and minds. The end of the matter, after we know about God in the revelation he has given in verbalized, propositional terms in the Scripture, is to be in relationship to him. A dead, ugly orthodoxy with no real spiritual reality must be rejected as sub-Christian.

Back in 1951 and '52, I went through a very deep time in

my own life. I had been a pastor for ten years and a missionary for another five, and I was connected with a group who stood very strongly for the truth of the Scriptures. But as I watched, it became clear to me that I saw very little spiritual reality. I had to ask why. I looked at myself as well and realized that my own spiritual reality was not as great as it had been immediately after my conversion. We were in Switzerland at that time, and I said to my wife, "I must really think this through."

I took about two months, and I walked in the mountains whenever it was clear. And when it was rainy, I walked back and forth in the hayloft over our chalet. I thought and wrestled and prayed, and I went all the way back to my agnosticism. I asked myself whether I had been right to stop being an agnostic and to become a Christian. I told my wife, if it didn't turn out right I was going to be honest and go back to America and put it all aside and do some other work.

I came to realize that indeed I had been right in becoming a Christian. But then I went on further and wrestled deeper and asked, "But then, where is the spiritual reality, Lord, among most of that which calls itself orthodoxy?" And gradually I found something. I found something that I had not been taught, a simple thing but profound. I discovered the meaning of the work of Christ, the meaning of the blood of Christ, moment by moment in our lives after we are Christians—the moment-by-moment work of the whole Trinity in our lives, because as Christians we are indwelt by the Holy Spirit. That is true spirituality.

I went out to Dakota, and I spoke at a Bible conference.

And the Lord used it and there was a real moving of God in that place. I preached it back in Switzerland. And gradually it became the book *True Spirituality*; and I want to tell you with all my heart that I think we could have had all the intellectual answers in the world at L'Abri, but if it had not been for those battles in which God gave me some knowledge of some spiritual reality in those days, not just theoretically but, poor as it was, knowledge of a relationship with God moment by moment on the basis of the blood of Jesus Christ, I don't believe there ever would have been a L'Abri.

Do we minimize the intellectual? I have just pled for the intellectual. I have pled for the propositional. I have pled against doctrinal compromises, specifically at the point of the Word of God being less than propositional truth all the way back to the first verse of Genesis. But at the same time there must be spiritual reality.

Will it be perfect? No, I do not believe the Bible ever holds out to us that anybody is perfect in this life. But it can be real, and it must be shown in some poor way. I say *poor* because I am sure when we get to heaven and look back, we will all see how poor it has been. And yet there must be some reality. There must be something real of the work of Christ in the moment-by-moment life, something real of the forgiveness of specific sin brought under the blood of Christ, something real in Christ's bearing his fruit through me through the indwelling of the Holy Spirit. These things must be there. There is nothing more ugly in all the world, nothing which more turns people aside, than a dead orthodoxy.

This, then, is the first reality, real spiritual reality.

Second Reality: The Beauty of Human Relationships

The second reality is the beauty of human relationships. True Christianity produces beauty as well as truth, especially in the specific areas of human relationships. Read the New Testament carefully with this in mind; notice how often Jesus returns us to this theme, how often Paul speaks of it. We are to show something to the watching world on the basis of the human relationships we have with other men, not just other Christians.

Christians today are the people who understand who man is. Modern man is in a dilemma because he does not know that man is qualitatively different from non-man. We say man is different because he is made in the image of God. But we must not say man is made in the image of God unless we look to God and by God's grace treat every man with dignity. We stand against B. F. Skinner in his book *Beyond Freedom and Dignity*. But I dare not argue against Skinner's determinism if I then treat the men I meet day by day as less than really made in the image of God.

I am talking first of all about non-Christians. The first commandment is to love the Lord our God with all our heart and soul and mind, and the second is to love our neighbor as ourselves. After Jesus commanded this, someone said, "Who is my neighbor?" And Jesus then told the story of the good Samaritan. He was not just talking about treating Christians well; he was talking about treating every man we meet well, every man whether he is in our social stratum or not, every man whether he speaks our language or not, every man whether he has the color of our skin or not. Every man is to be treated on the level of truly being made in the image of God, and thus there is to be a beauty of human relationships.

This attitude is to operate on all levels. I meet a man in a revolving door. How much time do I have with him? Maybe ten seconds. I am to treat him well. We look at him. We do not think consciously in every case that this man is made in the image of God, but, having ground into our bones and into our consciousness (as well as our doctrinal statement) that he is made in the image of God, we will treat him well in those ten seconds which we have.

We approach a red light. We have the same problem. Perhaps we will never see these other people at the intersection again, but we are to remember that they have dignity.

And when we come to the longer relationships, for example, the employer-employee relationship, we are to treat each person with dignity.[2] The husband-and-wife relationship, the parent-and-child relationship, the political relationship, the economic relationship—in every single relationship of life to the extent to which I am in contact with a man or woman, sometimes shorter and sometimes longer, he or she is to be treated in such a way that—man or woman—if he is thinking at all, he will say, "Didn't he treat me well!"

What about the liberal theologian? Yes, we are to stand against his theology. We are to practice truth, and we are not to compromise. We are to stand in antithesis to his theology. But even though we cannot cooperate with him

---

[2]The appendix to the present essay treats this topic in more detail.

in religious things, we are to treat the liberal theologian in such a way that we try from our side to bring our discussion into the circle of truly human relationships. Can we do these two things together in our own strength? No, but in the strength of the power of the Holy Spirit it can be done. We can have the beauty of human relationships even when we must say no.

Now, if we are called upon to love our neighbor as ourselves when he is not a Christian, how much more—ten thousand times ten thousand times more—should there be beauty in the relationships between true Bible-believing Christians, something so beautiful that the world would be brought up short! We must hold our distinctives. Some of us are Baptists; some of us hold to infant baptism; some of us are Lutheran and so on. But to true Bible-believing Christians across all the lines, in all the camps, I emphasize: If we do not show beauty in the way we treat each other, then in the eyes of the world and in the eyes of our own children, we are destroying the truth we proclaim.

Every big company, if it is going to build a huge plant, first makes a pilot plant in order to show that their plan will work. Every church, every mission, every Christian school, every Christian group, regardless of what sphere it is in, should be a pilot plant that the world can look at and see there a beauty of human relationships which stands in exact contrast to the awful ugliness of what modern men paint in their art, what they make with their sculpture, what they show in their cinema and how they treat each other. Men should see in the church a bold alternative to the way modern men treat people as animals and machines.

There should be something so different that they will listen, something so different it will commend the gospel to them.

Every group ought to be like that, and our relationships between our groups ought to be like that. Have they been? The answer all too often is no. We have something to ask the Lord to forgive us for. Evangelicals, we who are true Bible-believing Christians, must ask God to forgive us for the ugliness with which we have often treated each other when we are in different camps.

I am talking now about *beauty* and I have chosen this word with care. I could call it *love*, but we have so demoted the word that it is often meaningless. So I use the word *beauty*. There should be beauty, observable beauty, for the world to see in the way all true Christians treat each other.

We need two orthodoxies: first, an orthodoxy of doctrine and, second, an orthodoxy of community. Why was the early church able, within one century, to spread from the Indus River to Spain? Think of that: one century, India to Spain. When we read in Acts and in the Epistles, we find a church that *had* and *practiced* both orthodoxies (doctrine and community), and this could be observed by the world. Thus they commended the gospel to the world of that day and the Holy Spirit was not grieved.

There is a tradition (it is not in the Bible) that the world said about the Christians in the early church, "Behold, how they love each other." As we read Acts and the Epistles we realize that these early Christians were really struggling for a practicing community. We realize that one of the marks of the early church was a real community, a community that reached down all the way to their care for each other in their material needs.

Have we exhibited this community in our evangelical churches? I want to say no, by and large, no. Our churches have often been two things—preaching points and activity generators. When a person really has desperate needs in the area of race, or economic matters, or psychological matters, does he naturally expect to find a supporting community in our evangelical churches? We must say with tears, many times no!

My favorite church in Acts and, I guess, in all of history is the church at Antioch. I love the church at Antioch. I commend to you to read again about it. It was a place where something new happened: The great, proud Jews who despised the Gentiles (there was an anti-Gentilism among the Jews, just as so often, unhappily, there has been anti-Semitism among Gentiles) came to a breakthrough. They could not be silent. They told their Gentile neighbors about the Gospel, and suddenly, on the basis of the blood of Christ and the truth of the Word of God, the racial thing was solved. There were Jewish Christians and there were Gentile Christians and they were one!

More than that, there was a total span of the social spectrum. We are not told specifically that there were slaves in the church of Antioch, but we know there were in other places and there is no reason to think they were not in Antioch. We know by the record in Acts that there was no less a person in that church than Herod's foster brother. The man at the very peak of the social pyramid and the man at the bottom of the pile met together in the church of the

Lord Jesus Christ, and they were one in a beauty of human relationships.

And I love it for another reason. There was a man called Niger in that church, and that means black. More than likely he was a black man. The church at Antioch on the basis of the blood of Christ encompassed the whole. There was a beauty that the Greek and the Roman world did not know—and the world looked. And then there was the preaching of the gospel. In one generation the church spread from the Indus River to Spain. If we want to touch our generation, we must be no less than this.

I would emphasize again that community reached all the way down into the realm of material possessions. There is no *communism*, as we today know the word *communism*, in the book of Acts. Peter made very plain to Ananias and Sapphira that their land was their own and when they had sold their land they were masters of what they did with the money. No state or church law, no legalism, bound them. What existed in the early church was a love that was so overwhelming that they could not imagine in the church of the Lord Jesus having one man hungry and one man rich. When the Corinthian church fell into this, Paul was scathing in 1 Corinthians in writing against it.

Note, too, that deacons were appointed. Why? Because the church had found difficulty in caring for one another's material needs. Read James 1. James asks, "What are you doing preaching the gospel to a man and trying to have a good relationship with him spiritually if he needs shoes and you do not give him shoes?" Here is another place where this awful platonic element in the evangelical church has been so dominant and so deadly. It has been considered spiritual to give for missions but not equally spiritual to give when my brother needs shoes. That is never found in the Word of God. Of course the early church gave to missions; at times they gave money so Paul did not have to make tents. But Paul makes no distinction between collections for missions and collections for material needs, as if one were spiritual and the other not. For the most part when Paul spoke of financial matters, he did so because there was a group of Christians somewhere who had a material need and Paul then called upon other churches to help.

Moreover, it was not only in the local church that the Christians cared for each other's needs; they did so at great distances. The church of Macedonia, which was made up of Gentile Christians, when they heard that the Jewish Christians, the Jews whom they would previously have despised, had material need, took an offering and sent it with care hundreds of miles in order that the Jewish Christians might eat.

So, there must be two orthodoxies: the orthodoxy of doctrine and the orthodoxy of community. And both orthodoxies must be practiced down into the warp and the woof of life where the lordship of the Lord Jesus touches every area of our life.

Thus there are four requirements if we are to meet the needs of our generation. They are the two contents and then the two realities. And when there are the two contents and the two realities, we will begin to see something profound happen in our generation.

Appendix
Race and Economics

If I were writing my early books again (for example, *The God Who Is There* and *The Church at the End of the 20th Century*), I would make one change.

I would continue to emphasize that previously in the Northern European culture (including the United States) the controlling consensus was Christian, and that this is now changed and we live in a post-Christian world. However, in doing this I would point out that previously, when the Christian consensus was the controlling factor, certain things were definitely sub-Christian.

Christians of all people should have opposed any form of racism. We know from the Bible that all men have a unity because we have a common origin—we had a common ancestor. The "Christian" slave-owner should have known he was dealing with his own kind for two reasons. First, he should have known it when he had sexual intercourse with his female slave and she produced a child; this would not have happened had he performed bestiality with one of his animals. Second, he should have heard the message of a common ancestor not only taught but applied in a practical way in the Sunday-morning sermon. This applies to slavery, but it applies equally to any oppression or feeling of superiority on the basis of race.

Liberal theologians do not believe in the historicity of a

common ancestor, and the orthodox, conservatives, or evangelicals all too often did not courageously preach the practical conclusion of the fact of a common ancestor. The evangelical taught the doctrine of loving one's neighbor as oneself but failed to apply the lesson in the context in which Christ taught it, namely, in the setting of race—the Jew and the Samaritan. This lack discredits the Christian consensus and dishonors Christ.

The second point, no less wrong and destructive, is the lack of emphasis on the proper use of accumulated wealth. In a world of fallen, sinful men, the use of wealth has always been a problem that the true Christian should face, but it came to a point of special intensity with the Industrial Revolution and the rise of modern capitalism. Happily we can look back to some orthodox Christians, especially in England, who as a part of the preaching of the Gospel saw, preached and stood for the proper use of accumulated wealth. But, to our shame, the majority of the Church, when it was providing the consensus, was silent. Christians did not see that a failure to preach and act upon a compassionate use of accumulated wealth not only caused the Church to lose credibility with the working man but was actually a betrayal of a very important part of the biblical message. This fault was not confined to yesterday: It is still with us in many evangelical circles.

The Bible does clearly teach the right of property, but both the Old Testament and the New Testament put a tremendous stress on the compassionate use of that property.

If at each place where the employer was a Bible-believing Christian the world could see that less profit was being taken so that the workers would have appreciably more than the "going rate" of pay, the Gospel would have been better proclaimed throughout the whole world than if the profits were the same as the world took and then large endowments were given to Christian schools, missions and other projects. This is not to minimize the centrality of preaching the Gospel to the whole world, nor to minimize missions; it is to say that the other is also a way to proclaim the good news.

Unhappily, at our moment of history, in almost each place where true Christians are now speaking in this area, the tendency is to minimize missions and the preaching of the Gospel and/or to move over to some degree to the left. On the left, the solution is thought to be the state's becoming stronger in economic matters. But this is not the answer. Yes, the industrial complex is a threat, but why should Christians think that if modern men with their presuppositions use these lesser monolithic monsters to oppress, these same men (or others with the same presuppositions) would do otherwise with the greater monolithic monster of a bloated state?

The answer is where it should have been always, and especially since the Industrial Revolution: namely, in calling for a compassionate use of wealth by all who have it and especially by *the practice of* a compassionate use of wealth wherever true Christians are.

We must say we are sorry for the defectiveness of the preaching and the practice in these two areas, and we must make the proper emphasis concerning these an integral part of our evangelicalism.